Pericles

Plutarch

Kessinger Publishing's Rare Reprints

Thousands of Scarce and Hard-to-Find Books on These and other Subjects!

- Americana
- Ancient Mysteries
- Animals
- Anthropology
- Architecture
- Arts
- Astrology
- Bibliographies
- Biographies & Memoirs
- Body, Mind & Spirit
- Business & Investing
- Children & Young Adult
- Collectibles
- Comparative Religions
- Crafts & Hobbies
- Earth Sciences
- Education
- Ephemera
- Fiction
- Folklore
- Geography
- Health & Diet
- History
- Hobbies & Leisure
- Humor
- Illustrated Books
- Language & Culture
- Law
- Life Sciences
- Literature
- Medicine & Pharmacy
- Metaphysical
- Music
- Mystery & Crime
- Mythology
- Natural History
- Outdoor & Nature
- Philosophy
- Poetry
- Political Science
- Science
- Psychiatry & Psychology
- Reference
- Religion & Spiritualism
- Rhetoric
- Sacred Books
- Science Fiction
- Science & Technology
- Self-Help
- Social Sciences
- Symbolism
- Theatre & Drama
- Theology
- Travel & Explorations
- War & Military
- Women
- Yoga
- *Plus Much More!*

We kindly invite you to view our catalog list at:
http://www.kessinger.net

Because this article has been extracted from a parent book, it may have non-pertinent text at the beginning or end of it.

Any blank pages following the article are necessary for our book production requirements. The article herein is complete.

PERICLES

CÆSAR[1] once, seeing some wealthy strangers at Rome, carrying up and down with them in their arms and bosoms young puppy-dogs and monkeys, embracing and making much of them, took occasion not unnaturally to ask whether the women in their country were not used to bear children; by that prince-like reprimand gravely reflecting upon persons who spend and lavish upon brute beasts that affection and kindness which nature has implanted in us to be bestowed on those of our own kind. With like reason may we blame those who misuse that love of inquiry and observation which nature has implanted in our souls, by expending it on objects unworthy of the attention either of their eyes or their ears, while they disregard such as are excellent in themselves, and would do them good.

The mere outward sense, being passive in responding to the impression of the objects that come in its way and strike upon it, perhaps cannot help entertaining and taking notice of every thing that addresses it, be it what it will, useful or unuseful; but, in the exercise of his mental perception, every man, if he chooses, has a natural power to turn himself upon all occasions, and to change and shift with the greatest ease to what he shall himself judge desirable. So that it becomes a man's duty to pursue and make after the best and choicest of everything, that he may not only employ his contemplation, but may also be improved by it. For as that color is most suitable to the eye whose freshness and pleasantness stimulates and strengthens the sight, so a man ought to apply his intellectual perception to such objects as, with the sense of delight, are apt to call it forth, and allure it to its own proper good and advantage.

[1]Probably Augustus.

Such objects we find in the acts of virtue, which also produce in the minds of mere readers about them, an emulation and eagerness that may lead them on to imitation. In other things there does not immediately follow upon the admiration and liking of the thing done, any strong desire of doing the like. Nay, many times, on the very contrary, when we are pleased with the work, we slight and set little by the workman or artist himself, as, for instance, in perfumes and purple dyes, we are taken with the things themselves well enough, but do not think dyers and perfumers otherwise than low and sordid people. It was not said amiss by Antisthenes, when people told him that one Ismenias was an excellent piper, "It may be so," said he, "but he is but a wretched human being, otherwise he would not have been an excellent piper." And king Philip, to the same purpose, told his son Alexander, who once at a merry-meeting played a piece of music charmingly and skilfully, "Are you not ashamed, son, to play so well?" For it is enough for a king or prince to find leisure sometimes to hear others sing, and he does the muses quite honor enough when he pleases to be but present, while others engage in such exercises and trials of skill.

He who busies himself in mean occupations produces, in the very pains he takes about things of little or no use, an evidence against himself of his negligence and indisposition to what is really good. Nor did any generous and ingenuous young man, at the sight of the statue of Jupiter at Pisa, ever desire to be a Phidias, or, on seeing that of Juno at Argos, long to be a Polycletus, or feel induced by his pleasure in their poems to wish to be an Anacreon or Philetas or Archilochus. For it does not necessarily follow, that, if a piece of work please for its gracefulness, therefore he that wrought it deserves our admiration. Whence it is that neither do such things really profit or advantage the beholders, upon the sight of which no zeal arises for the imitation of them, nor any impulse or inclination, which may prompt any desire or endeavor of doing the like. But virtue, by the bare statement of its actions, can so affect men's minds as to create at once both admiration of the things done and desire to imitate the doers of them. The goods of fortune we would possess and would enjoy; those of virtue we long to practise and exercise; we are content to receive the former from others, the latter we wish others to experience from us. Moral good is a practical stimulus; it is no sooner seen, than it inspires an impulse to practise; and influences the mind and character not by a mere imitation which we look at, but, by the statement of the fact, creates a moral purpose which we form.

And so we have thought fit to spend our time and pains in writing of the lives of famous persons; and have composed this tenth book upon that subject, containing the life of Pericles, and that of Fabius Maximus, who carried on the war against Hannibal, men alike, as in their other virtues and good parts, so especially in their mild and upright temper and demeanor, and in that capacity to bear the cross-grained humors of their fellow-citizens and colleagues in office which made them both most useful and serviceable to the interests of their countries. Whether we take a right aim at our intended purpose, it is left to the reader to judge by what he shall here find.

Pericles was of the tribe Acamantis, and the township Cholargus, of the noblest birth both on his father's and mother's side. Xanthippus, his father, who defeated the king of Persia's generals in the battle at Mycale, took to wife Agariste, the grandchild of Clisthenes, who drove out the sons of Pisistratus, and nobly put an end to their tyrannical usurpation, and moreover made a body of laws, and settled a model of government admirably tempered and suited for the harmony and safety of the people.

His mother, being near her time, fancied in a dream that she was brought to bed of a lion, and a few days after was delivered of Pericles, in other respects perfectly formed, only his head was somewhat longish and out of proportion. For which reason almost all the images and statues that were made of him have the head covered with a helmet, the workmen apparently being willing not to expose him. The poets of Athens called him *Schinocephalos*, or squill-head, from *schinos*, a squill, or sea-onion. One of the comic poets, Cratinus, in the Chirons, tells us that—

> Old Chronos once took queen Sedition to wife;
> Which two brought to life
> That tyrant far-famed,
> Whom the gods the supreme skull-compeller[2] have named.

And, in the Nemesis, addresses him—

> Come, Jove, thou *head* of gods.

And a second, Teleclides, says, that now, in embarrassment with political difficulties, he sits in the city,—

> Fainting underneath the load
> Of his own head; and now abroad,
> From his huge galley of a pate,
> Sends forth trouble to the state.

And a third, Eupolis, in the comedy called the Demi, in a series of questions about each of the demagogues, whom he makes in the play to come up from hell, upon Pericles being named last, exclaims,—

> And here by way of summary, now we've done,
> Behold, in brief, the heads of all in one.

The master that taught him music, most authors are agreed, was Damon (whose name, they say, ought to be pronounced with the first syllable short). Though Aristotle tells us that he was thoroughly practised in all accomplishments of this kind by Pythoclides. Damon, it is not unlikely, being a sophist, out of policy, sheltered himself under the profession of music to conceal from people in general his skill in other things, and under this pretence attended Pericles, the young athlete of politics, so to say, as his training-master in these exercises. Damon's lyre, however, did not prove altogether a successful blind; he was banished the country by ostracism for ten years, as a dangerous intermeddler and a favorer of arbitrary power, and, by this means, gave the stage occasion to play upon him. As, for instance, Plato, the comic poet, introduces a character, who questions him—

> Tell me, if you please,
> Since you're the Chiron who taught Pericles.

[2] Kephalegeretes, a play on Nephelegeretes, the cloud-compeller.

Pericles, also, was a hearer of Zeno, the Eleatic, who treated of natural philosophy in the same manner as Parmenides did, but had also perfected himself in an art of his own for refuting and silencing opponents in argument; as Timon of Phlius describes it,—

> Also the two-edged tongue of mighty Zeno, who,
> Say what one would, could argue it untrue.

But he that saw most of Pericles, and furnished him most especially with a weight and grandeur of sense, superior to all arts of popularity, and in general gave him his elevation and sublimity of purpose and of character, was Anaxagoras of Clazomenæ; whom the men of those times called by the name of Nous, that is, mind, or intelligence, whether in admiration of the great and extraordinary gift he displayed for the science of nature, or because that he was the first of the philosophers who did not refer the first ordering of the world to fortune or chance, nor to necessity or compulsion, but to a pure, unadulterated intelligence, which in all other existing mixed and compound things acts as a principle of discrimination, and of combination of like with like.

For this man, Pericles entertained an extraordinary esteem and admiration, and, filling himself with this lofty, and, as they call it, up-in-the-air sort of thought, derived hence not merely, as was natural, elevation of purpose and dignity of language, raised far above the base and dishonest buffooneries of mob-eloquence, but, besides this, a composure of countenance, and a serenity and calmness in all his movements, which no occurrence whilst he was speaking could disturb, a sustained and even tone of voice, and various other advantages of a similar kind, which produced the greatest effect on his hearers. Once, after being reviled and ill-spoken of all day long in his own hearing by some vile and abandoned fellow in the open market-place, where he was engaged in the despatch of some urgent affair, he continued his business in perfect silence, and in the evening returned home composedly, the man still dogging him at the heels, and pelting him all the way with abuse and foul language; and stepping into his house, it being this time dark, he ordered one of his servants to take a light, and to go along

with the man and see him safe home. Ion, it is true, the
dramatic poet, says that Pericles's manner in company was
somewhat over-assuming and pompous; and that into his
high bearing there entered a good deal of slightingness and
scorn of others; he reserves his commendation for Cimon's
ease and pliancy and natural grace in society. Ion, however,
who must needs make virtue, like a show of tragedies, in-
clude some comic scenes,[3] we shall not altogether rely upon;
Zeno used to bid those who called Pericles's gravity the
affectation of a charlatan, to go and affect the like themselves; inasmuch as this mere counterfeiting might in time
insensibly instil into them a real love and knowledge of those
noble qualities.

Nor were these the only advantages which Pericles derived
from Anaxagoras's acquaintance; he seems also to have become, by his instructions, superior to that superstition with
which an ignorant wonder at appearances, for example,
in the heavens possesses the minds of people unacquainted
with their causes, eager for the supernatural, and
excitable through an inexperience which the knowledge
of natural causes removes, replacing wild and timid
superstition by the good hope and assurance of an intelligent
piety.

There is a story, that once Pericles had brought to him
from a country farm of his, a ram's head with one horn, and
that Lampon, the diviner, upon seeing the horn grow strong
and solid out of the midst of the forehead, gave it as his
judgment, that, there being at that time two potent factions,
parties, or interests in the city, the one of Thucydides and
the other of Pericles, the government would come about to
that one of them in whose ground or estate this token or in-
dication of fate had shown itself. But that Anaxagoras,
cleaving the skull in sunder, showed to the bystanders that
the brain had not filled up its natural place, but being oblong,
like an egg, had collected from all parts of the vessel which
contained it, in a point to that place from whence the root of
the horn took its rise. And that, for that time, Anaxagoras

[3]Three tragedies represented in succession were followed by a burlesque,
the so-called *satyric* drama, which has no connection, it must be remembered,
with the moral satire of the Romans, but takes its name from the grotesque
satyrs of the Greek woods.

was much admired for his explanation by those that were present; and Lampon no less a little while after, when Thucydides was overpowered, and the whole affairs of the state and government came into the hands of Pericles.

And yet, in my opinion, it is no absurdity to say that they were both in the right, both natural philosopher and diviner, one justly detecting the cause of this event, by which it was produced, the other the end for which it was designed. For it was the business of the one to find out and give an account of what it was made, and in what manner and by what means it grew as it did; and of the other to foretell to what end and purpose it was so made, and what it might mean or portend. Those who say that to find out the cause of a prodigy is in effect to destroy its supposed signification as such, do not take notice that, at the same time, together with divine prodigies, they also do away with signs and signals of human art and concert, as, for instance, the clashings of quoits, firebeacons, and the shadows on sun-dials, every one of which things has its cause, and by that cause and contrivance is a sign of something else. But these are subjects, perhaps, that would better befit another place.

Pericles, while yet but a young man, stood in considerable apprehension of the people, as he was thought in face and figure to be very like the tyrant Pisistratus, and those of great age remarked upon the sweetness of his voice, and his volubility and rapidity in speaking, and were struck with amazement at the resemblance. Reflecting, too, that he had a considerable estate, and was descended of a noble family, and had friends of great influence, he was fearful all this might bring him to be banished as a dangerous person; and for this reason meddled not at all with state affairs, but in military service showed himself of a brave and intrepid nature. But when Aristides was now dead, and Themistocles driven out, and Cimon was for the most part kept abroad by the expeditions he made in parts out of Greece, Pericles, seeing things in this posture, now advanced and took his side, not with the rich and few, but with the many and poor, contrary to his natural bent, which was far from democratical; but, most likely, fearing he might fall under suspicion of aiming at arbitrary power, and seeing Cimon on the side of the aristocracy, and much beloved by the better and more distinguished people, he joined the party of the people, with a view at once both to secure himself and procure means against Cimon.

He immediately entered, also, on quite a new course of life and management of his time. For he was never seen to walk in any street but that which led to the market-place and the council-hall, and he avoided invitations of friends to supper, and all friendly visiting and intercourse whatever; in all the time he had to do with the public, which was not a little, he was never known to have gone to any of his friends to a supper, except that once when his near kinsman Euryptolemus married, he remained present till the ceremony of the drink-offering,[4] and then immediately rose from table and went his way. For these friendly meetings are very quick to defeat any assumed superiority, and in intimate familiarity an exterior of gravity is hard to maintain. Real excellence, indeed, is most recognized when most openly looked into; and in really good men, nothing which meets the eyes of external observers so truly deserves their admiration, as their daily common life does that of their nearer friends. Pericles, however, to avoid any feeling of commonness, or any satiety on the part of the people, presented himself at intervals only, not speaking to every business, nor at all times coming into the assembly, but, as Critolaus says, reserving himself, like the Salaminian galley,[5] for great occasions, while matters of lesser importance were despatched by friends or other speakers under his direction. And of this number we are told Ephialtes made one, who broke the power of the council of Areopagus, giving the people, according to Plato's expression, so copious and so strong a draught of liberty, that, growing wild and unruly, like an unmanageable horse, it, as the comic poets say,—

"—— got beyond all keeping in,
Champing at Eubœa, and among the islands leaping in."

[4] The *spondai*, or libations, which, like the modern grace, concluded the meal, and were followed by the dessert.

[5] The Salaminia and the Paralus were the two sacred state-galleys of Athens, used only on special missions.

The style of speaking most consonant to his form of life and the dignity of his views he found, so to say, in the tones of that instrument with which Anaxagoras had furnished him; of his teaching he continually availed himself, and deepened the colors of rhetoric with the dye of natural science. For having, in addition to his great natural genius, attained, by the study of nature, to use the words of the divine Plato, this height of intelligence, and this universal consummating power, and drawing hence whatever might be of advantage to him in the art of speaking, he showed himself far superior to all others. Upon which account, they say, he had his nickname given him, though some are of opinion he was named the Olympian from the public buildings with which he adorned the city; and others again, from his great power in public affairs, whether of war or peace. Nor is it unlikely that the confluence of many attributes may have conferred it on him. However, the comedies represented at the time, which, both in good earnest and in merriment, let fly many hard words at him, plainly show that he got that appellation especially from his speaking; they speak of his "thundering and lightning" when he harangued the people, and of his wielding a dreadful thunderbolt in his tongue.

A saying also of Thucydides, the son of Melesias, stands on record, spoken by him by way of pleasantry upon Pericles's dexterity. Thucydides was one of the noble and distinguished citizens, and had been his greatest opponent; and, when Archidamus, the king of the Lacedæmonians, asked him whether he or Pericles were the better wrestler, he made this answer: "When I," said he, "have thrown him and given him a fair fall, by persisting that he had no fall, he gets the better of me, and makes the bystanders, in spite of their own eyes, believe him." The truth, however, is, that Pericles himself was very careful what and how he was to speak, insomuch that, whenever he went up to the hustings, he prayed the gods that no one word might unawares slip from him unsuitable to the matter and the occasion.

He has left nothing in writing behind him, except some decrees; and there are but very few of his sayings recorded; one, for example, is, that he said Ægina must, like a gather-

ing in a man's eye, be removed from Piræus; and another,
that he said he saw already war moving on its way towards
them out of Peloponnesus. Again, when on a time Sophocles,
who was his fellow-commissioner in the generalship, was
going on board with him, and praised the beauty of a youth
they met with in the way to the ship, "Sophocles," said he,
"a general ought not only to have clean hands, but also clean
eyes." And Stesimbrotus tells us, that, in his encomium on
those who fell in battle at Samos, he said they were become
immortal, as the gods were. "For," said he, "we do not see
them themselves, but only by the honors we pay them, and
by the benefits they do us, attribute to them immortality;
and the like attributes belong also to those that die in the
service of their country."

Since Thucydides describes the rule of Pericles as an
aristocratical government, that went by the name of a
democracy, but was, indeed, the supremacy of a single great
man, while many others say, on the contrary, that by him
the common people were first encouraged and led on to such
evils as appropriations of subject territory; allowances for
attending theatres, payments for performing public duties,
and by these bad habits were, under the influence of his public measures, changed from a sober, thrifty people, that
maintained themselves by their own labors, to lovers of
expense, intemperance, and license, let us examine the cause
of this change by the actual matters of fact.

At the first, as has been said, when he set himself against
Cimon's great authority, he did caress the people. Finding
himself come short of his competitor in wealth and money,
by which advantages the other was enabled to take care of
the poor, inviting every day some one or other of the citizens
that was in want to supper, and bestowing clothes on the
aged people, and breaking down the hedges and enclosures
of his grounds, that all that would might freely gather what
fruit they pleased, Pericles, thus outdone in popular arts,
by the advice of one Damonides of Œa, as Aristotle states,
turned to the distribution of the public moneys; and in a
short time having bought the people over, what with moneys
allowed for shows and for service on juries, and what with
other forms of pay and largess, he made use of them against

the council of Areopagus, of which he himself was no member, as having never been appointed by lot either chief archon, or lawgiver, or king, or captain.[6] For from of old these offices were conferred on persons by lot, and they who had acquitted themselves duly in the discharge of them were advanced to the court of Areopagus. And so Pericles, having secured his power and interest with the populace, directed the exertions of his party against this council with such success, that most of those causes and matters which had been used to be tried there, were, by the agency of Ephialtes, removed from its cognizance. Cimon, also, was banished by ostracism as a favorer of the Lacedæmonians and a hater of the people, though in wealth and noble birth he was among the first, and had won several most glorious victories over the barbarians, and had filled the city with money and spoils of war; as is recorded in the history of his life. So vast an authority had Pericles obtained among the people.

The ostracism was limited by law to ten years; but the Lacedæmonians, in the mean time, entering with a great army into the territory of Tanagra, and the Athenians going out against them, Cimon, coming from his banishment before his time was out, put himself in arms and array with those of his fellow-citizens that were of his own tribe, and desired by his deeds to wipe off the suspicion of his favoring the Lacedæmonians, by venturing his own person along with his countrymen. But Pericles's friends, gathering in a body, forced him to retire as a banished man. For which cause also Pericles seems to have exerted himself more in that than in any battle, and to have been conspicuous above all for his exposure of himself to danger. All Cimon's friends, also, to a man, fell together side by side, whom Pericles had accused with him of taking part with the Lacedæmonians. Defeated in this battle on their own frontiers, and expecting a new and perilous attack with return of spring, the Athenians now felt regret and sorrow for the loss of Cimon, and repentance

---

[6] Eponymus, Thesmothetes, Basileus, Polemarchus; titles of the different archons, the chief civic dignitaries, who, after the period of the Persian wars, were appointed, not by election, but simply by lot, from the whole body of citizens. Hence, at this time, the importance of the board of the ten *strategi*, or generals who were elected, and were always persons of real or supposed capacity.

for their expulsion of him. Pericles, being sensible of their feelings, did not hesitate or delay to gratify it, and himself made the motion for recalling him home. He, upon his return, concluded a peace betwixt the two cities; for the Lacedæmonians entertained as kindly feelings towards him as they did the reverse towards Pericles and the other popular leaders.

Yet some there are who say that Pericles did not propose the order for Cimon's return till some private articles of agreement had been made between them, and this by means of Elpinice, Cimon's sister; that Cimon, namely, should go out to sea with a fleet of two hundred ships, and be commander-in-chief abroad, with a design to reduce the king of Persia's territories, and that Pericles should have the power at home.

This Elpinice, it was thought, had before this time procured some favor for her brother Cimon at Pericles's hands, and induced him to be more remiss and gentle in urging the charge when Cimon was tried for his life; for Pericles was one of the committee appointed by the commons to plead against him. And when Elpinice came and besought him in her brother's behalf, he answered, with a smile, "O Elpinice, you are too old a woman to undertake such business as this." But, when he appeared to impeach him, he stood up but once to speak, merely to acquit himself of his commission, and went out of court, having done Cimon the least prejudice of any of his accusers.

How, then, can one believe Idomeneus, who charges Pericles as if he had by treachery procured the murder of Ephialtes, the popular statesman, one who was his friend, and of his own party in all his political course, out of jealousy, forsooth, and envy of his great reputation? This historian, it seems, having raked up these stories, I know not whence, has befouled with them a man who, perchance, was not altogether free from fault or blame, but yet had a noble spirit, and a soul that was bent on honor; and where such qualities are, there can no such cruel and brutal passion find harbor or gain admittance. As to Ephialtes, the truth of the story, as Aristotle has told it, is this: that having made himself formidable to the oligarchical party, by being an uncompromising asserter of the people's rights in calling to account and prosecuting those who any way wronged them, his enemies, lying in wait for him, by the means of Aristodicus the Tanagræan, privately despatched him.

Cimon, while he was admiral, ended his days in the Isle of Cyprus. And the aristocratical party, seeing that Pericles was already before this grown to be the greatest and foremost man of all the city, but nevertheless wishing there should be somebody set up against him, to blunt and turn the edge of his power, that it might not altogether prove a monarchy, put forward Thucydides of Alopece, a discreet person, and a near kinsman of Cimon's, to conduct the opposition against him; who, indeed, though less skilled in warlike affairs than Cimon was, yet was better versed in speaking and political business, and keeping close guard in the city, and engaging with Pericles on the hustings, in a short time brought the government to an equality of parties. For he would not suffer those who were called the honest and good (persons of worth and distinction) to be scattered up and down and mix themselves and be lost among the populace, as formerly, diminishing and obscuring their superiority amongst the masses; but taking them apart by themselves and uniting them in one body, by their combined weight he was able, as it were upon the balance, to make a counterpoise to the other party.

For, indeed, there was from the beginning a sort of concealed split, or seam, as it might be in a piece of iron, marking the different popular and aristocratical tendencies; but the open rivalry and contention of these two opponents made the gash deep, and severed the city into the two parties of the people and the few. And so Pericles, at that time more than at any other, let loose the reins to the people, and made his policy subservient to their pleasure, contriving continually to have some great public show or solemnity, some banquet, or some procession or other in the town to please them, coaxing his countrymen like children, with such delights and pleasures as were not, however, unedifying. Besides that every year he sent out three-score galleys, on board of which there went numbers of the citizens, who were in pay eight months, learning at the same time and practising the art of seamanship.

He sent, moreover, a thousand of them into the Chersonese as planters, to share the land among them by lot, and five hundred more into the isle of Naxos, and half that number to Andros, a thousand into Thrace to dwell among the Bisaltæ, and others into Italy, when the city Sybaris, which now was called Thurii, was to be repeopled. And this he did to ease and discharge the city of an idle, and, by reason of their idleness, a busy, meddling crowd of people; and at the same time to meet the necessities and restore the fortunes of the poor townsmen, and to intimidate, also, and check their allies from attempting any change, by posting such garrisons, as it were, in the midst of them.

That which gave most pleasure and ornament to the city of Athens, and the greatest admiration and even astonishment to all strangers, and that which now is Greece's only evidence that the power she boasts of and her ancient wealth are no romance or idle story, was his construction of the public and sacred buildings. Yet this was that of all his actions in the government which his enemies most looked askance upon and cavilled at in the popular assemblies, crying out how that the commonwealth of Athens had lost its reputation and was ill-spoken of abroad for removing the common treasure of the Greeks from the isle of Delos into their own custody; and how that their fairest excuse for so doing, namely, that they took it away for fear the barbarians should seize it, and on purpose to secure it in a safe place, this Pericles had made unavailable, and how that "Greece cannot but resent it as an insufferable affront, and consider herself to be tyrannized over openly, when she sees the treasure, which was contributed by her upon a necessity for the war, wantonly lavished out by us upon our city, to gild her all over, and to adorn and set her forth, as it were some vain woman, hung round with precious stones and figures and temples, which cost a world of money."

Pericles, on the other hand, informed the people, that they were in no way obliged to give any account of those moneys to their allies, so long as they maintained their defence, and kept off the barbarians from attacking them; while in the mean time they did not so much as supply one horse or man or ship, but only found money for the service;

"which money," said he, "is not theirs that give it, but theirs that receive it, if so be they perform the conditions upon which they receive it." And that it was good reason, that, now the city was sufficiently provided and stored with all things necessary for the war, they should convert the overplus of its wealth to such undertakings, as would hereafter, when completed, give them eternal honor, and, for the present, while in process, freely supply all the inhabitants with plenty. With their variety of workmanship and of occasions for service, which summon all arts and trades and require all hands to be employed about them, they do actually put the whole city, in a manner, into state-pay; while at the same time she is both beautified and maintained by herself. For as those who are of age and strength for war are provided for and maintained in the armaments abroad by their pay out of the public stock, so, it being his desire and design that the undisciplined mechanic multitude that stayed at home should not go without their share of public salaries, and yet should not have them given them for sitting still and doing nothing, to that end he thought fit to bring in among them, with the approbation of the people, these vast projects of buildings and designs of works, that would be of some continuance before they were finished, and would give employment to numerous arts, so that the part of the people that stayed at home might, no less than those that were at sea or in garrisons or on expeditions, have a fair and just occasion of receiving the benefit and having their share of the public moneys.

The materials were stone, brass, ivory, gold, ebony, cypress-wood; and the arts or trades that wrought and fashioned them were smiths and carpenters, moulders, founders and braziers, stone-cutters, dyers, goldsmiths, ivory-workers, painters, embroiderers, turners; those again that conveyed them to the town for use, merchants and mariners and shipmasters by sea, and by land, cartwrights, cattle-breeders, waggoners, rope-makers, flax-workers, shoe-makers and leather-dressers, road-makers, miners. And every trade in the same nature, as a captain in an army has his particular company of soldiers under him, had its own hired company of journeymen and laborers belonging to it banded together as in array, to be as it were the instrument and body for the performance of the service. Thus, to say all in a word, the occasions and services of these public works distributed plenty through every age and condition.

As then grew the works up, no less stately in size than exquisite in form, the workmen striving to outvie the material and the design with the beauty of their workmanship, yet the most wonderful thing of all was the rapidity of their execution. Undertakings, any one of which singly might have required, they thought, for their completion, several successions and ages of men, were every one of them accomplished in the height and prime of one man's political service. Although they say, too, that Zeuxis once, having heard Agatharchus the painter boast of despatching his work with speed and ease, replied, "I take a long time." For ease and speed in doing a thing do not give the work lasting solidity or exactness of beauty; the expenditure of time allowed to a man's pains beforehand for the production of a thing is repaid by way of interest with a vital force for its preservation when once produced. For which reason Pericles's works are especially admired, as having been made quickly, to last long. For every particular piece of his work was immediately, even at that time, for its beauty and elegance, antique; and yet in its vigor and freshness looks to this day as if it were just executed. There is a sort of bloom of newness upon those works of his, preserving them from the touch of time, as if they had some perennial spirit and undying vitality mingled in the composition of them.

Phidias had the oversight of all the works, and was surveyor-general, though upon the various portions other great masters and workmen were employed. For Callicrates and Ictinus built the Parthenon; the chapel at Eleusis, where the mysteries were celebrated, was begun by Corœbus, who erected the pillars that stand upon the floor or pavement, and joined them to the architraves; and after his death Metagenes of Xypete added the frieze and the upper line of columns; Xenocles of Cholargus roofed or arched the lantern on the top of the temple of Castor and Pollux; and the long wall, which Socrates says he himself heard Pericles propose

to the people, was undertaken by Callicrates. This work
Cratinus ridicules, as long in finishing,—

> 'Tis long since Pericles, if words would do it,
> Talk'd up the wall; yet adds not one mite to it.

The Odeum, or music-room, which in its interior was full
of seats and ranges of pillars, and outside had its roof made
to slope and descend from one single point at the top, was
constructed, we are told, in imitation of the king of Persia's
Pavilion; this likewise by Pericles's order; which Cratinus
again, in his comedy called The Thracian Women, made an
occasion of raillery,—

> So, we see here,
> Jupiter Long-pate Pericles appear,
> Since ostracism time, he's laid aside his head,
> And wears the new Odeum in its stead.

Pericles, also, eager for distinction, then first obtained the
decree for a contest in musical skill to be held yearly at the
Panathenæa, and he himself, being chosen judge, arranged
the order and method in which the competitors should sing
and play on the flute and on the harp. And both at that
time, and at other times also, they sat in this music-room to
see and hear all such trials of skill.

The propylæa, or entrances to the Acropolis, were finished
in five years' time, Mnesicles being the principal architect.
A strange accident happened in the course of building, which
showed that the goddess was not averse to the work, but
was aiding and coöperating to bring it to perfection. One
of the artificers, the quickest and the handiest workman
among them all, with a slip of his foot fell down from a
great height, and lay in a miserable condition, the physicians
having no hopes of his recovery. When Pericles was in
distress about this, Minerva appeared to him at night in a
dream, and ordered a course of treatment, which he applied,
and in a short time and with great ease cured the man. And
upon this occasion it was that he set up a brass statue of
Minerva, surnamed Health, in the citadel near the altar,
which they say was there before. But it was Phidias who
wrought the goddess's image in gold, and he has his name

inscribed on the pedestal as the workman of it; and indeed
the whole work in a manner was under his charge, and he
had, as we have said already, the oversight over all the artists
and workmen, through Pericles's friendship for him; and
this, indeed, made him much envied, and his patron shame-
fully slandered with stories, as if Phidias were in the habit
of receiving, for Pericles's use, freeborn women that came
to see the works. The comic writers of the town, when
they had got hold of this story, made much of it, and be-
spattered him with all the ribaldry they could invent, charging
him falsely with the wife of Menippus, one who was his
friend and served as lieutenant under him in the wars; and
with the birds kept by Pyrilampes, an acquaintance of Pericles, who, they pretended, used to give presents of peacocks
to Pericles's female friends. And how can one wonder at
any number of strange assertions from men whose whole
lives were devoted to mockery, and who were ready at any
time to sacrifice the reputation of their superiors to vulgar
envy and spite, as to some evil genius, when even Stesimbrotus the Thasian has dared to lay to the charge of Pericles
a monstrous and fabulous piece of criminality with his son's
wife? So very difficult a matter is it to trace and find out
the truth of any thing by history, when, on the one hand,
those who afterwards write it find long periods of time inter-
cepting their view, and, on the other hand, the contemporary
records of any actions and lives, partly through envy and
ill-will, partly through favor and flattery, pervert and distort
truth.

When the orators, who sided with Thucydides and his
party, were at one time crying out, as their custom was,
against Pericles, as one who squandered away the public
money, and made havoc of the state revenues, he rose in the
open assembly and put the question to the people, whether
they thought that he had laid out much; and they saying,
"Too much, a great deal," "Then," said he, "since it is so,
let the cost not go to your account, but to mine; and let the
inscription upon the buildings stand in my name." When
they heard him say thus, whether it were out of a surprise
to see the greatness of his spirit, or out of emulation of the
glory of the works, they cried aloud, bidding him to spend

on, and lay out what he thought fit from the public purse, and to spare no cost, till all were finished.

At length, coming to a final contest with Thucydides, which of the two should ostracize the other out of the country, and having gone through this peril, he drew his antagonist out, and broke up the confederacy that had been organized against him. So that now all schism and division being at an end, and the city brought to evenness and unity, he got all Athens and all affairs that pertained to the Athenians into his own hands, their tributes, their armies, and their galleys, the islands, the sea, and their wide-extended power, partly over other Greeks and partly over barbarians, and all that empire, which they possessed, founded and fortified upon subject nations and royal friendships and alliances.

After this he was no longer the same man he had been before, nor as tame and gentle and familiar as formerly with the populace, so as readily to yield to their pleasures and to comply with the desires of the multitude, as a steersman shifts with the winds. Quitting that loose, remiss, and, in some cases, licentious court of the popular will, he turned those soft and flowery modulations to the austerity of aristocratical and regal rule; and employing this uprightly and undeviatingly for the country's best interests, he was able generally to lead the people along, with their own wills and consents, by persuading and showing them what was to be done; and sometimes, too, urging and pressing them forward extremely against their will, he made them, whether they would or no, yield submission to what was for their advantage. In which, to say the truth, he did but like a skilful physician, who, in a complicated and chronic disease, as he sees occasion, at one while allows his patient the moderate use of such things as please him, at another while gives him keen pains and drugs to work the cure. For there arising and growing up, as was natural, all manner of distempered feelings among a people which had so vast a command and dominion, he alone, as a great master, knowing how to handle and deal fitly with each one of them, and, in an especial manner, making that use of hopes and fears, as his two chief rudders, with the one to check the career of their confidence at any time, with the other to raise them up and cheer them when under any discouragement, plainly showed by this, that rhetoric, or the art of speaking, is, in Plato's language, the government of the souls of men, and that her chief business is to address the affections and passions, which are as it were the strings and keys to the soul, and require a skilful and careful touch to be played on as they should be. The source of this predominance was not barely his power of language, but, as Thucydides assures us, the reputation of his life, and the confidence felt in his character; his manifest freedom from every kind of corruption, and superiority to all considerations of money. Notwithstanding he had made the city Athens, which was great of itself, as great and rich as can be imagined, and though he were himself in power and interest more than equal to many kings and absolute rulers, who some of them also bequeathed by will their power to their children, he, for his part, did not make the patrimony his father left him greater than it was by one drachma.

Thucydides, indeed, gives a plain statement of the greatness of his power; and the comic poets, in their spiteful manner, more than hint at it, styling his companions and friends the new Pisistratidæ, and calling on him to abjure any intention of usurpation, as one whose eminence was too great to be any longer proportionable to and compatible with a democracy or popular government. And Teleclides says the Athenians had surrendered up to him—

The tribute of the cities, and with them, the cities too, to do with
    them as he pleases, and undo;
To build up, if he likes, stone walls around a town; and again, if so
    he likes, to pull them down;
Their treaties and alliances, power, empire, peace, and war, their
    wealth and their success forevermore.

Nor was all this the luck of some happy occasion; nor was it the mere bloom and grace of a policy that flourished for a season; but having for forty years together maintained the first place among statesmen such as Ephialtes and Leocrates and Myronides and Cimon and Tolmides and Thucydides were, after the defeat and banishment of Thucydides, for no less than fifteen years longer, in the exercise of one continuous unintermitted command in the office, to which he was annually reëlected, of General, he preserved his integrity unspotted; though otherwise he was not altogether idle or careless in looking after his pecuniary advantage; his paternal estate, which of right belonged to him, he so ordered that it might neither through negligence be wasted or lessened, nor yet, being so full of business as he was, cost him any great trouble or time with taking care of it; and put it into such a way of management as he thought to be the most easy for himself, and the most exact. All his yearly products and profits he sold together in a lump, and supplied his household needs afterward by buying every thing that he or his family wanted out of the market. Upon which account, his children, when they grew to age, were not well pleased with his management, and the women that lived with him were treated with little cost, and complained of his way of housekeeping, where every thing was ordered and set down from day to day, and reduced to the greatest exactness; since there was not there, as is usual in a great family and a plentiful estate, any thing to spare, or over and above; but all that went out or came in, all disbursements and all receipts, proceeded as it were by number and measure. His manager in all this was a single servant, Evangelus by name, a man either naturally gifted or instructed by Pericles so as to excel every one in this art of domestic economy.

All this, in truth, was very little in harmony with Anaxagoras's wisdom; if, indeed, it be true that he, by a kind of divine impulse and greatness of spirit, voluntarily quitted his house, and left his land to lie fallow and to be grazed by sheep like a common. But the life of a contemplative philosopher and that of an active statesman are, I presume, not the same thing; for the one merely employs, upon great and good objects of thought, an intelligence that requires no aid of instruments nor supply of any external materials; whereas the other, who tempers and applies his virtue to human uses, may have occasion for affluence, not as a matter of mere necessity, but as a noble thing; which was Pericles's case, who relieved numerous poor citizens.

However, there is a story, that Anaxagoras himself, while

Pericles was taken up with public affairs, lay neglected, and
that, now being grown old, he wrapped himself up with a
resolution to die for want of food; which being by chance
brought to Pericles's ear, he was horror-struck, and instantly
ran thither, and used all the arguments and entreaties he
could to him, lamenting not so much Anaxagoras's condition
as his own, should he lose such a counsellor as he had found
him to be; and that, upon this, Anaxagoras unfolded his
robe, and showing himself, made answer: "Pericles," said
he, "even those who have occasion for a lamp supply it
with oil."

The Lacedæmonians beginning to show themselves troubled
at the growth of the Athenian power, Pericles, on the other
hand, to elevate the people's spirit yet more, and to raise
them to the thought of great actions, proposed a decree, to
summon all the Greeks in what part soever, whether of
Europe or Asia, every city, little as well as great, to send
their deputies to Athens to a general assembly, or conven-
tion, there to consult and advise concerning the Greek temples which the barbarians had burnt down, and the sacrifices
which were due from them upon vows they had made to their
gods for the safety of Greece when they fought against
the barbarians; and also concerning the navigation of the
sea, that they might henceforward all of them pass to and
fro and trade securely, and be at peace among themselves.

Upon this errand, there were twenty men, of such as were
above fifty years of age, sent by commission; five to summon
the Ionians and Dorians in Asia, and the islanders as far
as Lesbos and Rhodes; five to visit all the places in the
Hellespont and Thrace, up to Byzantium; and other five
besides these to go to Bœotia and Phocis and Peloponnesus,
and from hence to pass through the Locrians over to the
neighboring continent, as far as Acarnania and Ambracia;
and the rest to take their course through Eubœa to the
Œtæans and the Malian Gulf, and to the Achæans of
Phthiotis and the Thessalians; all of them to treat with the
people as they passed, and to persuade them to come and
take their part in the debates for settling the peace and
jointly regulating the affairs of Greece.

Nothing was effected, nor did the cities meet by their

deputies, as was desired; the Lacedæmonians, as it is said, crossing the design underhand, and the attempt being disappointed and baffled first in Peloponnesus. I thought fit, however, to introduce the mention of it, to show the spirit of the man and the greatness of his thoughts.

In his military conduct, he gained a great reputation for wariness; he would not by his good-will engage in any fight which had much uncertainty or hazard; he did not envy the glory of generals whose rash adventures fortune favored with brilliant success, however they were admired by others; nor did he think them worthy his imitation, but always used to say to his citizens that, so far as lay in his power, they should continue immortal, and live forever. Seeing Tolmides, the son of Tolmæus, upon the confidence of his former successes, and flushed with the honor his military actions had procured him, making preparation to attack the Bœotians in their own country, when there was no likely opportunity, and that he had prevailed with the bravest and most enterprising of the youth to enlist themselves as volunteers in the service, who besides his other force made up a thousand, he endeavored to withhold him and to advise him from it in the public assembly, telling him in a memorable saying of his, which still goes about, that, if he would not take Pericles's advice, yet he would not do amiss to wait and be ruled by time, the wisest counsellor of all. This saying, at that time, was but slightly commended; but within a few days after, when news was brought that Tolmides himself had been defeated and slain in battle near Coronea, and that many brave citizens had fallen with him, it gained him great repute as well as good-will among the people, for wisdom and for love of his countrymen.

But of all his expeditions, that to the Chersonese gave most satisfaction and pleasure, having proved the safety of the Greeks who inhabited there. For not only by carrying along with him a thousand fresh citizens of Athens he gave new strength and vigor to the cities, but also by belting the neck of land, which joins the peninsula to the continent, with bulwarks and forts from sea to sea, he put a stop to the inroads of the Thracians, who lay all about the Chersonese, and closed the door against a continual and grievous war,

with which that country had been long harassed, lying ex-
posed to the encroachments and influx of barbarous neighbors,
and groaning under the evils of a predatory population both
upon and within its borders.

Nor was he less admired and talked of abroad for his
sailing round the Peloponnesus, having set out from Pegæ,
or The Fountains, the port of Megara, with a hundred galleys. For he not only laid waste the sea-coast, as Tolmides
had done before, but also, advancing far up into main land
with the soldiers he had on board, by the terror of his
appearance drove many within their walls; and at Nemea,
with main force, routed and raised a trophy over the Sicyo-
nians, who stood their ground and joined battle with him.
And having taken on board a supply of soldiers into the
galleys, out of Achaia, then in league with Athens, he crossed
with the fleet to the opposite continent, and, sailing along by
the mouth of the river Achelous, overran Acarnania, and
shut up the Œniadæ within their city walls, and having
ravaged and wasted their country, weighed anchor for home
with the double advantage of having shown himself formidable to his enemies, and at the same time safe and energetic
to his fellow-citizens; for there was not so much as any
chance-miscarriage that happened, the whole voyage through,
to those who were under his charge.

Entering also the Euxine Sea with a large and finely
equipped fleet, he obtained for the Greek cities any new
arrangements they wanted, and entered into friendly relations
with them; and to the barbarous nations, and kings and
chiefs round about them, displayed the greatness of the power
of the Athenians, their perfect ability and confidence to sail
wherever they had a mind, and to bring the whole sea under
their control. He left the Sinopians thirteen ships of war,
with soldiers under the command of Lamachus, to assist them
against Timesileus the tyrant; and when he and his accom-
plices had been thrown out, obtained a decree that six
hundred of the Athenians that were willing should sail to
Sinope and plant themselves there with the Sinopians, sharing
among them the houses and land which the tyrant and his
party had previously held.

But in other things he did not comply with the giddy

impulses of the citizens, nor quit his own resolutions to follow
their fancies, when, carried away with the thought of their
strength and great success, they were eager to interfere
again in Egypt, and to disturb the king of Persia's maritime
dominions. Nay, there were a good many who were, even
then, possessed with that unblest and inauspicious passion
for Sicily, which afterward the orators of Alcibiades's party
blew up into a flame. There were some also who dreamt of
Tuscany and of Carthage, and not without plausible reason
in their present large dominion and the prosperous course
of their affairs.

But Pericles curbed this passion for foreign conquest, and
unsparingly pruned and cut down their ever busy fancies
for a multitude of undertakings; and directed their power
for the most part to securing and consolidating what they
had already got, supposing it would be quite enough for
them to do, if they could keep the Lacedæmonians in check;
to whom he entertained all along a sense of opposition;
which, as upon many other occasions, so he particularly
showed by what he did in the time of the holy war. The
Lacedæmonians, having gone with an army to Delphi, restored Apollo's temple, which the Phocians had got into their
possession, to the Delphians; immediately after their departure, Pericles, with another army, came and restored the
Phocians. And the Lacedæmonians having engraven the
record of their privilege of consulting the oracle before
others, which the Delphians gave them, upon the forehead of
the brazen wolf which stands there, he, also, having received
from the Phocians the like privilege for the Athenians, had
it cut upon the same wolf of brass on his right side.

That he did well and wisely in thus restraining the exertions of the Athenians within the compass of Greece, the
events themselves that happened afterward bore sufficient
witness. For, in the first place, the Eubœans revolted,
against whom he passed over with forces; and then, immediately after, news came that the Megarians were turned
their enemies, and a hostile army was upon the borders of
Attica, under the conduct of Plistoanax, king of the Lacedæmonians. Wherefore Pericles came with his army back
again in all haste out of Eubœa, to meet the war which

threatened at home; and did not venture to engage a numerous and brave army eager for battle; but perceiving that Plistoanax was a very young man, and governed himself mostly by the counsel and advice of Cleandrides, whom the ephors had sent with him, by reason of his youth, to be a kind of guardian and assistant to him, he privately made trial of this man's integrity, and, in a short time, having corrupted him with money, prevailed with him to withdraw the Peloponnesians out of Attica. When the army had re· tired and dispersed into their several states, the Lacedæmonians in anger fined their king in so large a sum of money, that, unable to pay it, he quitted Lacedæmon; while Cleandrides fled, and had sentence of death passed upon him in his absence. This was the father of Gylippus, who overpowered the Athenians in Sicily. And it seems that this covetousness was an hereditary disease transmitted from father to son; for Gylippus also afterwards was caught in foul practices, and expelled from Sparta for it. But this we have told at large in the account of Lysander.

When Pericles, in giving up his accounts of this expedition, stated a disbursement of ten talents, as laid out upon fit occasion, the people, without any question, nor troubling themselves to investigate the mystery, freely allowed of it. And some historians, in which number is Theophrastus the philosopher, have given it as a truth that Pericles every year used to send privately the sum of ten talents to Sparta, with which he complimented those in office, to keep off the war; not to purchase peace neither, but time, that he might prepare at leisure, and be the better able to carry on war hereafter.

Immediately after this, turning his forces against the revolters, and passing over into the island of Eubœa with fifty sail of ships and five thousand men in arms, he reduced their cities, and drove out the citizens of the Chalcidians, called Hippobotæ, horse-feeders, the chief persons for wealth and reputation among them; and removing all the Histiæans out of the country, brought in a plantation of Athenians in their room; making them his one example of severity, because they had captured an Attic ship and killed all on board.

After this, having made a truce between the Athenians and Lacedæmonians for thirty years, he ordered, by public decree, the expedition against the Isle of Samos, on the ground, that, when they were bid to leave off their war with the Milesians, they had not complied. And as these measures against the Samians are thought to have been taken to please Aspasia, this may be a fit point for inquiry about the woman, what art or charming faculty she had that enabled her to captivate, as she did, the greatest statesmen, and to give the philosophers occasion to speak so much about her, and that, too, not to her disparagement. That she was a Milesian by birth, the daughter of Axiochus, is a thing acknowledged. And they say it was in emulation of Thargelia, a courtesan of the old Ionian times, that she made her addresses to men of great power. Thargelia was a great beauty, extremely charming, and at the same time sagacious: she had numerous suitors among the Greeks, and brought all who had to do with her over to the Persian interest, and by their means, being men of the greatest power and station, sowed the seeds of the Median faction up and down in several cities.[7] Aspasia, some say, was courted and caressed by Pericles upon account of her knowledge and skill in politics. Socrates himself would sometimes go to visit her, and some of his acquaintance with him; and those who frequented her company would carry their wives with them to listen to her. Her occupation was any thing but creditable, her house being a home for young courtesans. Æschines tells us also, that Lysicles, a sheep-dealer, a man of low birth and character, by keeping Aspasia company after Pericles's death, came to be a chief man in Athens. And in Plato's Menexenus, though we do not take the introduction as quite serious, still thus much seems to be historical, that she had the repute of being resorted to by many of the Athenians for instruction in the art of speaking. Pericles's inclination for her seems, however, to have rather proceeded from the passion of love. He had a wife that was near of kin to him, who had been married first to Hipponicus, by whom she had Callias, surnamed the Rich; and also she brought Pericles, while she lived with him, two sons, Xanthippus and Paralus. Afterwards, when they did not well agree nor like to live together,

[7] She was married, says Athenæus, to fourteen husbands; a woman of great beauty and intellect.

he parted with her, with her own consent, to another man, and himself took Aspasia, and loved her with wonderful affection; every day, both as he went out and as he came in from the market-place, he saluted and kissed her.

In the comedies she goes by the nicknames of the new Omphale and Deianira, and again is styled Juno. Cratinus, in downright terms, calls her a harlot.

> To find him a Juno the goddess of lust
> Bore that harlot past shame,
> Aspasia by name.

It should seem, also, that he had a son by her; Eupolis, in his Demi, introduced Pericles asking after his safety, and Myronides replying,

> "My son?" "He lives; a man he had been long,
> But that the harlot-mother did him wrong."

Aspasia, they say, became so celebrated and renowned, that Cyrus also, who made war against Artaxerxes for the Persian monarchy, gave her whom he loved the best of all his concubines the name of Aspasia, who before that was called Milto. She was a Phocæan by birth, the daughter of one Hermotimus, and, when Cyrus fell in battle, was carried to the king, and had great influence at court. These things coming into my memory as I am writing this story, it would be unnatural for me to omit them.

Pericles, however, was particularly charged with having proposed to the assembly the war against the Samians, from favor to the Milesians, upon the entreaty of Aspasia. For the two states were at war for the possession of Priene; and the Samians, getting the better, refused to lay down their arms and to have the controversy betwixt them decided by arbitration before the Athenians. Pericles, therefore, fitting out a fleet, went and broke up the oligarchical government at Samos, and, taking fifty of the principal men of the town as hostages, and as many of their children, sent them to the isle of Lemnos, there to be kept, though he had offers, as some relate, of a talent a piece for himself from each one of the hostages, and of many other presents from those who were anxious not to have a democracy. Moreover, Pissuthnes the Persian, one of the king's lieutenants, bearing some good-will to the Samians, sent him ten thousand pieces of gold to excuse the city. Pericles, however, would receive none of all this; but after he had taken that course with the Samians which he thought fit, and set up a democracy among them, sailed back to Athens.

But they, however, immediately revolted, Pissuthnes having privily got away their hostages for them, and pro- vided them with means for the war. Whereupon Pericles came out with a fleet a second time against them, and found them not idle nor slinking away, but manfully resolved to try for the dominion of the sea. The issue was, that, after a sharp sea-fight about the island called Tragia, Pericles ob- tained a decisive victory, having with forty-four ships routed seventy of the enemy's, twenty of which were carrying soldiers.

Together with his victory and pursuit, having made himself master of the port, he laid siege to the Samians, and blocked them up, who yet, one way or other, still ventured to make sallies, and fight under the city walls. But after that another greater fleet from Athens was arrived, and that the Samians were now shut up with a close leaguer on every side, Pericles, taking with him sixty galleys, sailed out into the main sea, with the intention, as most authors give the account, to meet a squadron of Phœnician ships that were coming for the Samians' relief, and to fight them at as great distance as could be from the island; but, as Stesimbrotus says, with a design of putting over to Cyprus; which does not seem to be probable. But whichever of the two was his intent, it seems to have been a miscalculation. For on his departure, Melis- sus, the son of Ithagenes, a philosopher, being at that time general in Samos, despising either the small number of the ships that were left or the inexperience of the commanders, prevailed with the citizens to attack the Athenians. And the Samians having won the battle, and taken several of the men prisoners, and disabled several of the ships, were masters of the sea, and brought into port all necessaries they wanted for the war, which they had not before. Aristotle says, too, that Pericles himself had been once before this worsted by this Melissus in a sea-fight.

The Samians, that they might requite an affront which had before been put upon them, branded the Athenians, whom they took prisoners, in their foreheads, with the figure of an owl. For so the Athenians had marked them before with a Samæna, which is a sort of ship, low and flat in the prow, so as to look snub-nosed, but wide and large and well-spread in the hold, by which it both carries a large cargo and sails well. And it was so called, because the first of that kind was seen at Samos, having been built by order of Polycrates the tyrant. These brands upon the Samians' foreheads, they say, are the allusion in the passage of Aristophanes, where he says,—

> For, oh, the Samians are a lettered people.

Pericles, as soon as news was brought him of the disaster that had befallen his army, made all the haste he could to come in to their relief, and having defeated Melissus, who bore up against him, and put the enemy to flight, he immediately proceeded to hem them in with a wall, resolving to master them and take the town, rather with some cost and time, than with the wounds and hazards of his citizens. But as it was a hard matter to keep back the Athenians, who were vexed at the delay, and were eagerly bent to fight, he divided the whole multitude into eight parts, and arranged by lot that that part which had the white bean should have leave to feast and take their ease, while the other seven were fighting. And this is the reason, they say, that people, when at any time they have been merry, and enjoyed themselves, call it white day, in allusion to this white bean.

Ephorus the historian tells us besides, that Pericles made use of engines of battery in this siege, being much taken with the curiousness of the invention, with the aid and presence of Artemon himself, the engineer, who, being lame, used to be carried about in a litter, where the works required his attendance, and for that reason was called Periphoretus. But Heraclides Ponticus disproves this out of Anacreon's poems, where mention is made of this Artemon Periphoretus several ages before the Samian war, or any of these occurrences. And he says that Artemon, being a man who loved his ease, and had a great apprehension of danger, for the most part kept close within doors, having two of his servants to hold a brazen shield over his head, that nothing might fall upon him from above; and if he were at any time forced upon necessity to go abroad, that he was carried about in a little hanging bed, close to the very ground, and that for this reason he was called Periphoretus.

In the ninth month, the Samians surrendering themselves and delivering up the town, Pericles pulled down their walls, and seized their shipping, and set a fine of a large sum of money upon them, part of which they paid down at once, and they agreed to bring in the rest by a certain time, and gave hostages for security. Duris the Samian makes a tragical drama out of these events, charging the Athenians and Pericles with a great deal of cruelty, which neither Thucydides, nor Ephorus, nor Aristotle have given any relation of, and probably with little regard to truth; how, for example, he brought the captains and soldiers of the galleys into the market-place at Miletus, and there having bound them fast to boards for ten days, then, when they were already all but half dead, gave order to have them killed by beating out their brains with clubs, and their dead bodies to be flung out into the open streets and fields, unburied. Duris, however, who even where he has no private feeling concerned, is not wont to keep his narrative within the limits of truth, is the more likely upon this occasion to have exaggerated the calamities which befell his country, to create odium against the Athenians. Pericles, however, after the reduction of Samos, returning back to Athens, took care that those who died in the war should be honorably buried, and made a funeral harangue, as the custom is, in their commendation at their graves, for which he gained great admiration. As he came down from the stage on which he spoke, the rest of the women came and complimented him, taking him by the hand, and crowning him with garlands and ribbons, like a victorious athlete in the games; but Elpinice, coming near to him, said, "These are brave deeds, Pericles, that you have done, and such as deserve our chaplets; who have lost us many a worthy citizen, not in a war with Phœnicians or Medes, like my brother Cimon, but for the overthrow of an allied and kindred city." As Elpinice spoke these words, he, smiling quietly, as it is said, returned her answer with this verse,—

Old women should not seek to be perfumed.

Ion says of him, that, upon this exploit of his, conquering the Samians, he indulged very high and proud thoughts of himself: whereas Agamemnon was ten years a-taking a barbarous city, he had in nine months' time vanquished and taken the greatest and most powerful of the Ionians. And indeed it was not without reason that he assumed this glory to himself, for, in real truth, there was much uncertainty and great hazard in this war, if so be, as Thucydides tells us, the Samian state were within a very little of wresting the whole power and dominion of the sea out of the Athenians' hands.

After this was over, the Peloponnesian war beginning to break out in full tide, he advised the people to send help to the Corcyræans, who were attacked by the Corinthians, and to secure to themselves an island possessed of great naval resources, since the Peloponnesians were already all but in actual hostilities against them. The people readily consenting to the motion, and voting an aid and succor for them, he despatched Lacedæmonius, Cimon's son, having only ten ships with him, as it were out of a design to affront him; for there was a great kindness and friendship betwixt Cimon's family and the Lacedæmonians; so, in order that Lacedæmonius might lie the more open to a charge, or suspicion at least, of favoring the Lacedæmonians and playing false, if he performed no considerable exploit in this service, he allowed him a small number of ships, and sent him out against his will; and indeed he made it somewhat his business to hinder Cimon's sons from rising in the state, professing that by their very names they were not to be looked upon as native and true Athenians, but foreigners and strangers, one being called Lacedæmonius, another Thessalus, and the third Eleus; and they were all three of them, it was thought, born of an Arcadian woman. Being, however, ill spoken of on account of these ten galleys, as having afforded but a small supply to the people that were in need, and yet given a great advantage to those who might complain of the act of intervention,

Pericles sent out a larger force afterward to Corcyra, which arrived after the fight was over. And when now the Corinthians, angry and indignant with the Athenians, accused them publicly at Lacedæmon, the Megarians joined with them, complaining that they were, contrary to common right and the articles of peace sworn to among the Greeks, kept out and driven away from every market and from all ports under the control of the Athenians. The Æginetans, also, professing to be ill-used and treated with violence, made supplications in private to the Lacedæmonians for redress, though not daring openly to call the Athenians in question. In the mean time, also, the city of Potidæa, under the dominion of the Athenians, but a colony formerly of the Corinthians, had revolted, and was beset with a formal siege, and was a further occasion of precipitating the war.

Yet notwithstanding all this, there being embassies sent to Athens, and Archidamus, the king of the Lacedæmonians, endeavoring to bring the greater part of the complaints and matters in dispute to a fair determination, and to pacify and allay the heats of the allies, it is very likely that the war would not upon any other grounds of quarrel have fallen upon the Athenians, could they have been prevailed with to repeal the ordinance against the Megarians, and to be reconciled to them. Upon which account, since Pericles was the man who mainly opposed it, and stirred up the people's passions to persist in their contention with the Megarians, he was regarded as the sole cause of the war.

They say, moreover, that ambassadors went, by order from Lacedæmon to Athens about this very business, and that when Pericles was urging a certain law which made it illegal to take down or withdraw the tablet of the decree, one of the ambassadors, Polyalces by name, said, "Well, do not take it down then, but *turn* it; there is no law, I suppose, which forbids that;"[8] which, though prettily said, did not move Pericles from his resolution. There may have been, in all likelihood, something of a secret grudge and private animosity which he had against the Megarians. Yet, upon a

---

[8] The word for *taking down*, in the literal sense, is also the technical term for revoking, or repealing; hence the Spartans play upon the two senses. "If you may not take it down, turn it, with its face to the wall."

public and open charge against them, that they had appropriated part of the sacred land on the frontier, he proposed a decree that a herald should be sent to them, and the same also to the Lacedæmonians, with an accusation of the Megarians; an order which certainly shows equitable and friendly proceeding enough. And after that the herald who was sent, by name Anthemocritus, died, and it was believed that the Megarians had contrived his death, then Charinus proposed a decree against them, that there should be an irreconcilable and implacable enmity thenceforward betwixt the two commonwealths; and that if any one of the Megarians should but set his foot in Attica, he should be put to death; and that the commanders, when they take the usual oath, should, over and above that, swear that they will twice every year make an inroad into the Megarian country; and that Anthemocritus should be buried near the Thriasian Gates, which are now called the Dipylon, or Double Gate.

On the other hand, the Megarians, utterly denying and disowning the murder of Anthemocritus, throw the whole matter upon Aspasia and Pericles, availing themselves of the famous verses in the Acharnians,

> To Megara some of our madcaps ran,
> And stole Simætha thence, their courtesan.
> Which exploit the Megarians to outdo,
> Came to Aspasia's house, and took off two.

The true occasion of the quarrel is not so easy to find out. But of inducing the refusal to annul the decree, all alike charge Pericles. Some say he met the request with a positive refusal, out of high spirit and a view of the state's best interests, accounting that the demand made in those embassies was designed for a trial of their compliance, and that a concession would be taken for a confession of weakness, as if they durst not do otherwise; while other some there are who say that it was rather out of arrogance and a wilful spirit of contention, to show his own strength, that he took occasion to slight the Lacedæmonians. The worst motive of all, which is confirmed by most witnesses, is to the following effect. Phidias the Moulder had, as has before been said, undertaken to make the statue of Minerva. Now he, being admitted to friendship with Pericles, and a great favorite of his, had many enemies upon this account, who envied and maligned him; who also, to make trial in a case of his, what kind of judges the commons would prove, should there be occasion to bring Pericles himself before them, having tampered with Menon, one who had been a workman with Phidias, stationed him in the market-place, with a petition desiring public security upon his discovery and impeachment of Phidias. The people admitting the man to tell his story, and the prosecution proceeding in the assembly, there was nothing of theft or cheat proved against him; for Phidias, from the very first beginning, by the advice of Pericles, had so wrought and wrapt the gold that was used in the work about the statue, that they might take it all off and make out the just weight of it, which Pericles at that time bade the accusers do. But the reputation of his works was what brought envy upon Phidias, especially that where he represents the fight of the Amazons upon the goddesses' shield, he had introduced a likeness of himself as a bald old man holding up a great stone with both hands, and had put in a very fine representation of Pericles fighting with an Amazon. And the position of the hand, which holds out the spear in front of the face, was ingeniously contrived to conceal in some degree the likeness, which, meantime, showed itself on either side.

Phidias then was carried away to prison, and there died of a disease; but, as some say, of poison, administered by the enemies of Pericles, to raise a slander, or a suspicion, at least, as though he had procured it. The informer Menon, upon Glycon's proposal, the people made free from payment of taxes and customs, and ordered the generals to take care that nobody should do him any hurt. About the same time, Aspasia was indicted of impiety, upon the complaint of Hermippus the comedian, who also laid further to her charge that she received into her house freeborn women for the uses of Pericles. And Diopithes proposed a decree, that public accusation should be laid against persons who neglected religion, or taught new doctrines about things above,[9]

[9]"Supera ac cœlestia," as Cicero translates the words *meteora* and *metarsia*, whence we have formed our *meteorology*. The whole Greek

directing suspicion, by means of Anaxagoras, against Pericles himself. The people receiving and admitting these accusations and complaints, at length, by this means, they came to enact a decree, at the motion of Dracontides, that Pericles should bring in the accounts of the moneys he had expended, and lodge them with the Prytanes; and that the judges, carrying their suffrage from the altar in the Acropolis, should examine and determine the business in the city. This last clause Hagnon took out of the decree, and moved that the causes should be tried before fifteen hundred jurors, whether they should be styled prosecutions for robbery, or bribery, or any kind of malversation. Aspasia, Pericles begged off, shedding, as Æschines says, many tears at the trial, and personally entreating the jurors. But fearing how it might go with Anaxagoras, he sent him out of the city. And finding that in Phidias's case he had miscarried with the people, being afraid of impeachment, he kindled the war, which hitherto had lingered and smothered, and blew it up into a flame; hoping, by that means, to disperse and scatter these complaints and charges, and to allay their jealousy; the city usually throwing herself upon him alone, and trusting to his sole conduct, upon the urgency of great affairs and public dangers, by reason of his authority and the sway he bore.

These are given out to have been the reasons which induced Pericles not to suffer the people of Athens to yield to the proposals of the Lacedæmonians; but their truth is uncertain.

The Lacedæmonians, for their part, feeling sure that if they could once remove him, they might be at what terms they pleased with the Athenians, sent them word that they should expel the "Pollution" with which Pericles on the mother's side was tainted, as Thucydides tells us. But the issue proved quite contrary to what those who sent the message expected; instead of bringing Pericles under suspicion and reproach, they raised him into yet greater credit and esteem with the citizens, as a man whom their enemies most hated and feared. In the same way, also, before Archidamus, who was at the head of the Peloponnesians, made his inva-

religion was based on certain conceptions of such phenomena, any tampering with which was, therefore, quickly resented.

sion into Attica, he told the Athenians beforehand, that if
Archidamus, while he laid waste the rest of the country,
should forbear and spare his estate, either on the ground
of friendship or right of hospitality that was betwixt them,
or on purpose to give his enemies an occasion of traducing
him, that then he did freely bestow upon the state all that
his land and the buildings upon it for the public use. The
Lacedæmonians, therefore, and their allies, with a great
army, invaded the Athenian territories, under the conduct of
king Archidamus, and laying waste the country, marched on
as far as Acharnæ, and there pitched their camp, presuming
that the Athenians would never endure that, but would come
out and fight them for their country's and their honor's sake.
But Pericles looked upon it as dangerous to engage in battle,
to the risk of the city itself, against sixty thousand men-at-
arms of Peloponnesians and Bœotians; for so many they
were in number that made the inroad at first; and he endeavored to appease those who were desirous to fight, and
were grieved and discontented to see how things went, and
gave them good words, saying, that "trees, when they are
lopped and cut, grow up again in a short time, but men, being
once lost, cannot easily be recovered." He did not convene
the people into an assembly, for fear lest they should force
him to act against his judgment; but, like a skilful steersman
or pilot of a ship, who, when a sudden squall comes on, out
at sea, makes all his arrangements, sees that all is tight and
fast, and then follows the dictates of his skill, and minds the
business of the ship, taking no notice of the tears and entreaties of the sea-sick and fearful passengers, so he, having
shut up the city gates, and placed guards at all posts for
security, followed his own reason and judgment, little regard-
ing those that cried out against him and were angry at his
management, although there were a great many of his friends
that urged him with requests, and many of his enemies
threatened and accused him for doing as he did, and many
made songs and lampoons upon him, which were sung about
the town to his disgrace, reproaching him with the cowardly
exercise of his office of general, and the tame abandonment
of everything to the enemy's hands.

Cleon, also, already was among his assailants, making use

of the feeling against him as a step to the leadership of the people, as appears in the anapæstic verses of Hermippus.

> Satyr-king, instead of swords,
> Will you always handle words?
> Very brave indeed we find them,
> But a Teles[10] lurks behind them.
>
> Yet to gnash your teeth you're seen,
> When the little dagger keen,
> Whetted every day anew,
> Of sharp Cleon touches you.

Pericles, however, was not at all moved by any attacks, but took all patiently, and submitted in silence to the disgrace they threw upon him and the ill-will they bore him; and, sending out a fleet of a hundred galleys to Peloponnesus, he did not go along with it in person, but stayed behind, that he might watch at home and keep the city under his own control, till the Peloponnesians broke up their camp and were gone. Yet to soothe the common people, jaded and distressed with the war, he relieved them with distributions of public moneys, and ordained new divisions of subject land. For having turned out all the people of Ægina, he parted the island among the Athenians, according to lot. Some comfort, also, and ease in their miseries, they might receive from what their enemies endured. For the fleet, sailing round the Peloponnese, ravaged a great deal of the country, and pillaged and plundered the towns and smaller cities; and by land he himself entered with an army the Megarian country, and made havoc of it all. Whence it is clear that the Peloponnesians, though they did the Athenians much mischief by land, yet suffering as much themselves from them by sea, would not have protracted the war to such a length, but would quickly have given it over, as Pericles at first foretold they would, had not some divine power crossed human purposes.

In the first place, the pestilential disease, or plague, seized upon the city, and ate up all the flower and prime of their youth and strength. Upon occasion of which, the people, distempered and afflicted in their souls, as well as in their

[10] Apparently some notorious coward.

bodies, were utterly enraged like madmen against Pericles, and, like patients grown delirious, sought to lay violent hands on their physician, or, as it were, their father. They had been possessed, by his enemies, with the belief that the occasion of the plague was the crowding of the country people together into the town, forced as they were now, in the heat of the summer-weather, to dwell many of them together even as they could, in small tenements and stifling hovels, and to be tied to a lazy course of life within doors, whereas before they lived in a pure, open, and free air. The cause and author of all this, said they, is he who on account of the war has poured a multitude of people from the country in upon us within the walls, and uses all these many men that he has here upon no employ or service, but keeps them pent up like cattle, to be overrun with infection from one another, affording them neither shift of quarters nor any refreshments.

With the design to remedy these evils, and do the enemy some inconvenience, Pericles got a hundred and fifty galleys ready, and having embarked many tried soldiers, both foot and horse, was about to sail out, giving great hope to his citizens, and no less alarm to his enemies, upon the sight of so great a force. And now the vessels having their complement of men, and Pericles being gone aboard his own galley, it happened that the sun was eclipsed, and it grew dark on a sudden, to the affright of all, for this was looked upon as extremely ominous. Pericles, therefore, perceiving the steersman seized with fear and at a loss what to do, took his cloak and held it up before the man's face, and, screening him with it so that he could not see, asked him whether he imagined there was any great hurt, or the sign of any great hurt in this, and he answering No, "Why," said he, "and what does that differ from this, only that what has caused that darkness there, is something greater than a cloak?" This is a story which philosophers tell their scholars. Pericles, however, after putting out to sea, seems not to have done any other exploit befitting such preparations, and when he had laid siege to the holy city Epidaurus, which gave him some hope of surrender, miscarried in his design by reason of the sickness. For it not only seized upon the Athenians, but upon all others, too, that held any sort of communica-

tion with the army. Finding after this the Athenians ill
affected and highly displeased with him, he tried and endeavored what he could to appease and re-encourage them.
But he could not pacify or allay their anger, nor persuade
or prevail with them any way, till they freely passed their
votes upon him, resumed their power, took away his command from him, and fined him in a sum of money; which,
by their account that say least, was fifteen talents, while
they who reckon most, name fifty. The name prefixed to the
accusation was Cleon, as Idomeneus tells us; Simmias, according to Theophrastus; and Heraclides Ponticus gives it
as Lacratidas.

After this, public troubles were soon to leave him unmo-
lested; the people, so to say, discharged their passion in their
stroke, and lost their stings in the wound. But his domestic
concerns were in an unhappy condition, many of his friends
and acquaintance having died in the plague time, and those
of his family having long since been in disorder and in a
kind of mutiny against him. For the eldest of his lawfully
begotten sons, Xanthippus by name, being naturally prodigal,
and marrying a young and expensive wife, the daughter of
Tisander, son of Epilycus, was highly offended at his father's
economy in making him but a scanty allowance, by little and
little at a time. He sent, therefore, to a friend one day, and
borrowed some money of him in his father Pericles's name,
pretending it was by his order. The man coming afterward
to demand the debt, Pericles was so far from yielding to pay
it, that he entered an action against him. Upon which the
young man, Xanthippus, thought himself so ill used and dis-
obliged, that he openly reviled his father; telling first, by
way of ridicule, stories about his conversations at home, and
the discourses he had with the sophists and scholars that
came to his house. As for instance, how one who was a prac-
tiser of the five games of skill,[11] having with a dart or javelin
unawares against his will struck and killed Epitimus the
Pharsalian, his father spent a whole day with Protagoras in
a serious dispute, whether the javelin, or the man that threw

[11]These are recorded in a pentameter verse by Simonides.

Halma, podokeiēn, discon, aconta, palēn.
Leaping, and swiftness of foot, wrestling, the discus, the dart.

it, or the masters of the games who appointed these sports,
were, according to the strictest and best reason, to be ac-
counted the cause of this mischance. Beside this, Stesimbrotus tells us that it was Xanthippus who spread abroad
among the people the infamous story concerning his own
wife; and in general that this difference of the young man's
with his father, and the breach betwixt them, continued never
to be healed or made up till his death. For Xanthippus died
in the plague time of the sickness. At which time Pericles
also lost his sister, and the greatest part of his relations and
friends, and those who had been most useful and serviceable
to him in managing the affairs of state. However, he did not
shrink or give in upon these occasions, nor betray or lower
his high spirit and the greatness of his mind under all his
misfortunes; he was not even so much as seen to weep or
to mourn, or even attend the burial of any of his friends or
relations, till at last he lost his only remaining legitimate
son. Subdued by this blow, and yet striving still, as far as
he could, to maintain his principle, and to preserve and keep
up the greatness of his soul, when he came, however, to perform the ceremony of putting a garland of flowers upon the
head of the corpse, he was vanquished by his passion at the
sight, so that he burst into exclamations, and shed copious
tears, having never done any such thing in all his life before.

The city having made trial of other generals for the conduct of war, and orators for business of state, when they
found there was no one who was of weight enough for such
a charge, or of authority sufficient to be trusted with so
great a command, regretted the loss of him, and invited him
again to address and advise them, and to reassume the office
of general. He, however, lay at home in dejection and
mourning; but was persuaded by Alcibiades and others of
his friends to come abroad and show himself to the people;
who having, upon his appearance, made their acknowledg-
ments, and apologized for their untowardly treatment of him,
he undertook the public affairs once more; and, being chosen
general, requested that the statute concerning base-born
children, which he himself had formerly caused to be made,
might be suspended; that so the name and race of his family
might not, for absolute want of a lawful heir to succeed, be

wholly lost and extinguished. The case of the statute was thus: Pericles, when long ago at the height of his power in the state, having then, as has been said, children lawfully begotten, proposed a law that those only should be reputed true citizens of Athens who were born of such parents as were both Athenians. After this, the king of Egypt having sent to the people, by way of present, forty thousand bushels of wheat, which were to be shared out among the citizens, a great many actions and suits about legitimacy occurred, by virtue of that edict; cases which, till that time, had not been known nor taken notice of; and several persons suffered by false accusations. There were little less than five thousand who were convicted and sold for slaves; those who, enduring the test, remained in the government and passed muster for true Athenians were found upon the poll to be fourteen thousand and forty persons in number.

It looked strange, that a law, which had been carried so far against so many people, should be cancelled again by the same man that made it; yet the present calamity and distress which Pericles labored under in his family broke through all objections, and prevailed with the Athenians to pity him, as one whose losses and misfortunes had sufficiently punished his former arrogance and haughtiness. His sufferings deserved, they thought, their pity, and even indignation, and his request was such as became a man to ask and men to grant; they gave him permission to enroll his son in the register of his fraternity, giving him his own name. This son afterward, after having defeated the Peloponnesians at Arginusæ, was, with his fellow-generals, put to death by the people.

About the time when his son was enrolled, it should seem, the plague seized Pericles, not with sharp and violent fits, as it did others that had it, but with a dull and lingering distemper, attended with various changes and alterations, leisurely, by little and little, wasting the strength of his body, and undermining the noble faculties of his soul. So that Theophrastus, in his Morals, when discussing whether men's characters change with their circumstances, and their moral habits, disturbed by the ailings of their bodies, start aside from the rules of virtue, has left it upon record, that Pericles, when he was sick, showed one of his friends that came to visit him, an amulet or charm that the women had hung about his neck; as much as to say, that he was very sick indeed when he would admit of such a foolery as that was.

When he was now near his end, the best of the citizens and those of his friends who were left alive, sitting about him, were speaking of the greatness of his merit, and his power, and reckoning up his famous actions and the number of his victories; for there were no less than nine trophies, which, as their chief commander and conqueror of their enemies, he had set up, for the honor of the city. They talked thus together among themselves, as though he were unable to understand or mind what they said, but had now lost his consciousness. He had listened, however, all the while, and attended to all, and speaking out among them, said, that he wondered they should commend and take notice of things which were as much owing to fortune as to any thing else, and had happened to many other commanders, and, at the same time, should not speak or make mention of that which was the most excellent and greatest thing of all. "For," said he, "no Athenian, through my means, ever wore mourning."

He was indeed a character deserving our high admiration, not only for his equitable and mild temper, which all along in the many affairs of his life, and the great animosities which he incurred, he constantly maintained; but also for the high spirit and feeling which made him regard it the noblest of all his honors that, in the exercise of such immense power, he never had gratified his envy or his passion, nor ever had treated any enemy as irreconcilably opposed to him. And to me it appears that this one thing gives that otherwise childish and arrogant title a fitting and becoming significance; so dispassionate a temper, a life so pure and unblemished, in the height of power and place, might well be called Olympian, in accordance with our conceptions of the divine beings, to whom, as the natural authors of all good and of nothing evil, we ascribe the rule and government of the world. Not as the poets represent, who, while confounding us with their ignorant fancies, are themselves confuted by their own poems and fictions, and call the place, indeed, where they say the gods make their abode, a secure and quiet seat, free from all hazards and commotions, untroubled with winds or with clouds, and equally through all time illumined with soft serenity and a pure light, as though such were a home most agreeable for a blessed and immortal nature; and yet, in the mean while, affirm that the gods themselves are full of trouble and enmity and anger and other passions, which no way become or belong to even men that have any understanding. But this will, perhaps, seem a subject fitter for some other consideration, and that ought to be treated of in some other place.

The course of public affairs after his death produced a quick and speedy sense of the loss of Pericles. Those who, while he lived, resented his great authority, as that which eclipsed themselves, presently after his quitting the stage, making trial of other orators and demagogues, readily acknowledged that there never had been in nature such a disposition as his was, more moderate and reasonable in the height of that state he took upon him, or more grave and impressive in the mildness which he used. And that invidious, arbitrary power, to which formerly they gave the name of monarchy and tyranny, did then appear to have been the chief bulwark of public safety; so great a corruption and such a flood of mischief and vice followed, which he, by keeping weak and low, had withheld from notice, and had prevented from attaining incurable height through a licentious impunity.

This is the end of this publication.

Any remaining blank pages are for our book binding
requirements and are blank on purpose.

To search thousands of interesting publications like this one,
please remember to visit our website at:

http://www.kessinger.net

www.ingramcontent.com/pod-product-compliance
Lightning Source LLC
LaVergne TN
LVHW091941060326
832903LV00043B/11